RICK WARREN

DVD Study Guide

God's Answers to Life's Difficult Questions

A Six-Session Video-Based Study for Groups or Individuals

ZONDERVAN

ZONDERVAN.com/
AUTHORTRACKER
follow your favorite authors

ZONDERVAN

God's Answers to Life's Difficult Questions Study Guide
Copyright © 2009 by Rick Warren

Requests for information should be addressed to:

Zondervan, *Grand Rapids, Michigan 49530*

ISBN 978-0-310-32692-2

13 14 15 · 24 23 22 21 20 19 18 17 16 15 14 13 12 11 10 9 8 7

CONTENTS

UNDERSTANDING YOUR STUDY GUIDE

Here is a brief explanation of the features of this study guide.

Looking Ahead/Catching Up: You will open each meeting with an opportunity for everyone to check in with each other about how you are doing with the weekly assignments. Accountability is a key to success in this study!

Key Verse: Each week you will find a key verse or Scripture passage for your group to read together. If someone in the group has a different translation, ask them to read it aloud so the group can get a bigger picture of the meaning of the passage.

Video Lessons: There is a video segment for the group to watch together each week. Take notes in the lesson outlines and fill in the blanks as you watch the video, and be sure to refer back to these notes during your discussion time.

Discovery Questions: Each video segment is complemented by questions for group discussion. Please don't feel pressured to discuss every single question. If you don't get through all of the discovery questions, that's okay. The material in this study is meant to be your servant, not your master, so there is no reason to rush through the answers. Give everyone ample opportunity to share their thoughts.

Living on Purpose: In his book, *The Purpose Driven® Life*, Rick Warren identifies God's five purposes for our lives. They are worship, fellowship, discipleship, ministry, and evangelism. We will focus on one or two of these five purposes in each lesson, and discuss how it relates to the subject of the study. This section is very important, so please be sure to leave time for it.

Prayer Direction: At the end of each session you will find suggestions for your group prayer time. Praying together is one of the greatest privileges of small group life. Please don't take it for granted.

Putting It into Practice: We don't want to be just hearers of the Word. We also need to be doers of the Word (James 1:22). This section of the study explains the assignments we would like you to complete before your next meeting. These assignments are application exercises that will help you put into practice the truths you have discussed in the lesson.

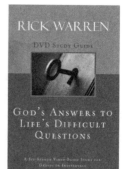

Diving Deeper: The material in this small group study is designed to complement the book, *God's Answers to Life's Difficult Questions*, by Rick Warren (Zondervan, 2006). Each week, this section will direct you to additional reading from the book for greater understanding of the topic.

How to Use
This Video Curriculum

Follow these five simple steps for a successful small group meeting:

1. Open your group meeting by using the "Looking Ahead" or "Catching Up" sections of your study guide.

2. Watch the video segment together and take notes in the outlines in this study guide. Each video segment is approximately twenty minutes in length.

3. Complete the rest of the discussion materials for each session, including the "Living on Purpose" and "Prayer Direction" sections.

4. Review the "Putting It into Practice" assignments and commit to doing them before your next meeting.

5. Read the book! To maximize the impact of this study, each participant should have a copy of both this study guide and the book, *God's Answers to Life's Difficult Questions*, by Rick Warren. Reading assignments and in-group review of chapters in the book are a vital part of this learning experience. The book will become a valuable, permanent resource for review and sharing once the course has been completed.

SESSION ONE

HOW CAN I COPE
WITH STRESS?

LOOKING AHEAD

- If your group is new or you have new members, take a few minutes to let everyone introduce themselves and share how they came to be part of this group.

- Share with the group why you are here. What is the one question you want God to answer in your life as a result of this study?

- In this first session, share what you would ask God if you had five minutes in person with him right now.

KEY VERSE

*Cast your cares on the L*ORD *and he will sustain you;*
he will never let the righteous fall.

Psalm 55:22 (NIV)

Watch the video now and fill in the blanks in your outline. Refer back to the outline during your discussion time.

SESSION ONE

How Can I Cope with Stress?

Introduction

Jesus summarized the secret of stress management when he said:

> 28 *"Come to me, all you who are weary and*
> *burdened, and I will give you rest.* 29 *Take my yoke*
> *upon you and learn from me, for I am gentle and*
> *humble in heart, and you will find rest for your*
> *souls.* 30 *For my yoke is easy and my burden is light."*
>
> Matthew 11:28–30 (NIV)

Three Keys to Stress Management

1. _____ **to Jesus**

- Jesus says, "I will give you rest for your souls." This is much

  deeper than physical rest. This is _____ .

  > 29 *He gives power to those who are tired and worn*
  > *out; he offers strength to the weak . . .* 31 *those who*
  > *wait on the LORD will find new strength.*
  >
  > Isaiah 40:29, 31 (NLT)

- The antidote for an overloaded soul is a _____ .

2. _____ **His Yoke**

If you want to lighten your load, you need to let go of control.

A yoke is a wooden beam that attaches two farm animals together. By sharing the load, they lighten the load.

• A yoke is a symbol of _____ .

> _Pile your troubles on God's shoulders—he'll carry your load, he'll help you out._
>
> Psalm 55:22 (MSG)

Jesus says, "Join up with me, connect with me, get attached to me, put on the yoke with me and I'll carry the load with you."

• A yoke is a symbol of _____ .

Oxen yoked together are controlled by the master; when you are yoked with Christ you are controlled by God.

• When you're yoked with Christ you move together in the same

   _____ and at the same _____ .

> _Since we live by the Spirit, let us keep in step with the Spirit._
>
> Galatians 5:25 (NIV)

> _Our lives get in step with God . . . by letting him set the pace, not by proudly or anxiously trying to run the parade._
>
> Romans 3:28 (MSG)

Who's setting the pace in your life right now? Let God be your pacesetter.

3. _____ **to Trust**

Learn to trust by following Jesus' model. Study how Jesus lived and do what he did, and you'll have the same kind of peace that Jesus had.

Learning is a process . . . it takes time. Your habits of a hurried, worried lifestyle didn't start yesterday, and they won't go away overnight. You've got to unlearn some old things. And you'll have to learn some new things from Jesus.

• Jesus' secret of peace: _____ to the Father.

If you are at the breaking point from overload, come to Jesus. Take up his yoke. Learn to trust. Let Jesus be your pacesetter and find rest for your soul.

DISCOVERY QUESTIONS

1. Rick asked, "Who's setting the pace for your life right now?" How would you answer that question?

2. Why do you think we tend to overload our schedules? What steps can help keep us from doing that in the future?

3. How can we take on Jesus' yoke? What does that look like to you?

4. In what area of your life do you need rest for your soul?

5. Where are you in learning to trust God? Share honestly with your group and ask for prayer to grow in this process.

LIVING ON PURPOSE

Discipleship

Jesus says, "I only do what the Father tells me to do." If Jesus only did what the Father did and what the Father said, then his pace was set by the Father. Examine the current pace of your life. If you desire to be like Christ, how is it possible? How can you hear what the Father is saying and do what he is telling you to do? How can you find and follow his pace for your life?

PRAYER DIRECTION

Admit to God that you are tired of being tired, and worn out with trying to control everything around you. Ask him to help you build margin in your life and to trust him more. Ask him to pour Christ's likeness into you, and be ready to receive it.

PUTTING IT INTO PRACTICE

Which of the three points Rick addressed for coping with stress caught your attention most? Do you need to:

1. Come to Jesus? Are you tired and worn out? Make a place in your schedule this next week to literally come to Jesus. Find that secluded place talked about in Matthew 6:6 and seek that soul rest only he can give you.

2. Take up his yoke? Maybe you've been carrying your own burdens so long you can barely stand up under their pressure. Surrender them now into his hands. Just say, "Lord, I'm sorry for trying to live life by my own power. Please take my problems, my burdens, and help me learn to depend on you." Now the trick is—you need to leave them with him. No taking them back!

3. Learn to trust him? Remember it's a process, learned over time. Keep in mind Jesus' model of doing only what the Father told him to do. Seek to live a life of obedience. You won't regret it.

Focus on one of these three points this week, and share your progress at your next group meeting.

DIVING DEEPER

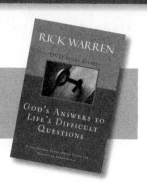

Read Chapter 1 of *God's Answers to Life's Difficult Questions*.

HOW CAN I
REBOUND FROM FAILURE?

CATCHING UP

- Share one idea from last week's session that stayed with you the most this past week. What were you able to put into practice?

- Has God ever helped you bounce back from a place of failure? Share your story briefly as an encouragement for the group.

KEY VERSE

And we know that in all things God works for the
good of those who love him . . .

Romans 8:28 (NIV)

Watch the video now and fill in the blanks in this lesson outline. Refer back to the outline during your discussion time.

SESSION TWO

How Can I Rebound from Failure?

Introduction

The only way to never fail is to never try anything new. Failure is a part of life. If you don't fail, then you're not really trying. If you want to rebound from a failure, you must first get over the fear of failing again.

> *25 "'I was afraid and went out and hid your talent in the ground . . .' 26His master replied, 'You wicked, lazy servant!'"*
>
> Matthew 25:25–26 (NIV)

That's what God thinks when we play it safe and refuse to take risks, when we refuse to live by faith. You cannot become what God wants you to be by playing it safe.

How to Overcome the Fear of Failure

1. Remember _____

The failure rate of human beings is 100 percent. Nobody is perfect.

> *We all stumble in many ways.*
>
> James 3:2 (NIV)

2. Remember Failure Is _____

The fear of failure is worse than failure itself.

> *For though a righteous man falls seven times, he*
> *rises again . . .*
>
> Proverbs 24:16 (NIV)

History books are filled with biographies of people who failed, got up, kept going, and eventually succeeded.

> *And let us not get tired of doing what is right, for*
> *after a while we will reap a harvest of blessing if we*
> *don't get discouraged and give up.*
>
> Galatians 6:9 (LB)

3. Recognize the _____ of Failure

> *And we know that in all things God works for the*
> *good of those who love him . . .*
>
> Romans 8:28 (NIV)

"All things" includes failure.

Benefits of Failure:

- Failure _____ .

- Failure develops _____ .

- Failure helps us _____ .

- Failure makes us _____ .

4. _____ Failure

Failure is not falling short of your dream—failure is not even having a dream to begin with.

> *I have done my best in the race, I have run the full distance, and I have kept the faith.*
>
> 2 Timothy 4:7 (GNT)

5. _____ Yourself to Others

> *Let everyone... [do] his very best, for then he will have the personal satisfaction of work done well and won't need to compare himself with someone else.*
>
> Galatians 6:4 (LB)

Success is doing your best. Failure is not making the effort. When you compare yourself with others you set yourself up for the fear of failure.

6. Replace Fear with _____

> *I have the strength to face all conditions by the power that Christ gives me.*
>
> Philippians 4:13 (GNT)

How to Become a Follower of Christ

Have you ever surrendered your life to Jesus Christ?
Take a few minutes with your group to watch a brief video by
Pastor Rick Warren on how to become part of the family of God.
It is included on the Session Two menu of this DVD.

DISCOVERY QUESTIONS

1. What does failure mean to you? Talk about a hard failure in your life. What did it feel like? What did you learn from it?

2. Why do you think failure is discouraging when it happens? Share a time when you or someone you know benefited as a result of failure. How can that example help you get past failure to try again?

3. Since everyone fails—including superstars and heroes of history—what is it that makes successful people different?

4. Romans 8:28 says, "And we know that in all things God works for the good of those who love him" (NIV), and Galatians 6:9 instructs us, "And let us not get tired of doing what is right, for after a while we will reap a harvest of blessing if we don't get discouraged and give up" (LB). Which phrase from these two verses speaks most directly to you?

LIVING ON PURPOSE

Ministry

Involvement in ministry has a way of taking our minds off our own problems as we look to the needs of others. How do you think a ministry that offers practical service—like Meals on Wheels, holding a church service for shut-ins, or working with a local rescue mission—could help you rebound from failure? Share your ideas with your group and then make a plan to do something about it this week, either as a remedy for a current situation or as reinforcement for the future. Be prepared to share with your group next week the step you took toward ministry.

PRAYER DIRECTION

Pray for one another's needs, remembering to ask God for his vision in your life. What risk in ministry or evangelism does he want you to take? As his disciple, thank him for the fact that taking risks always results in growth, and ask him to hold your hand as you plan to take a risk for him.

PUTTING IT INTO PRACTICE

Rick said, "The only way to never fail is to never try anything new." Like the childhood advice to get right back on the bike after you fall off, sometimes the best way to rebound from failure is to try something new—take a risk! This week, plan to take some God-glorifying, God-honoring risks—like inviting to church that neighbor, coworker, or family member who's been on your heart. Be prepared to share the results with your group. Remember—if your invitation is rejected it doesn't mean you have failed. You have been obedient and that is all God asks. The rest is up to him.

DIVING DEEPER

Read chapter 2 of *God's Answers to Life's Difficult Questions.*

SESSION THREE

HOW CAN I
BE CONFIDENT IN A CRISIS?

CATCHING UP

- What step did you take toward ministry or what new risk did you take this past week?

- Is there an area of your life where you need more confidence? Express that need to your group as you begin this lesson.

KEY VERSES

Have no fear of sudden disaster . . . for the Lord
will be your confidence . . .

Proverbs 3:25–26 (NIV)

Watch the video now and fill in the blanks in this lesson outline. Refer back to the outline during your discussion time.

How Can I Be Confident in a Crisis?

Introduction

> *25Have no fear of sudden disaster . . . 26for the LORD will be your confidence . . .*
>
> Proverbs 3:25–26 (NIV)

God doesn't want you to be fearful when you face a crisis. He wants you to be confident.

Jesus Calms the Storm

> *23Then [Jesus] got into the boat and his disciples followed him. 24Without warning, a furious storm came up on the lake, so that the waves swept over the boat. But Jesus was sleeping. 25The disciples went and woke him, saying, "Lord, save us! We're going to drown!" 26He replied, "You of little faith, why are you so afraid?" Then he got up and rebuked the winds and the waves, and it was completely calm. 27The men were amazed and asked, "What kind of man is this? Even the winds and the waves obey him!"*
>
> Matthew 8:23–27 (NIV)

FIVE FACTS ABOUT CRISES

1. Crises Are _____

James 1:2 says, "When you face trials . . ." not if, but when.

2. Crises Are _____

There are many kinds of crises: situational, relational, emotional, financial . . .

3. Crises Are _____

> *"He . . . sends rain on the righteous and the unrighteous."*
>
> Matthew 5:45 (NIV)

They happen to both good people and bad people. They can even happen when you're doing the right thing.

4. Crises Are _____

> *Without warning, a furious storm came up . . .*
>
> Matthew 8:24 (NIV)

5. I Can _____ to Crises

You basically have two options when you face a crisis: You can be filled with panic, like the disciples, or you can be filled with peace like Jesus.

> *[24][When the] storm came up . . . the waves swept over the boat . . . [25]The disciples went and woke [Jesus] saying, "Lord, save us! We're going to drown!"*
>
> Matthew 8:24–25 (NIV)

How Can I Have Peace in a Crisis?

• Refocus on _____ .

Get your eyes off the crisis and onto Christ.

> *Then [Jesus] got into the boat and his disciples*
> *followed him.*
>
> Matthew 8:23 (NIV)

The disciples forgot that God was in the boat. When we go through trials and crises, we tend to think we're all alone. The Bible says we are not.

> *¹"Fear not, for I have redeemed you; I have [called]*
> *you by name, you are mine. ²When you pass*
> *through the waters, I will be with you; and when*
> *you pass through the rivers, they will not sweep*
> *over you . . ."*
>
> Isaiah 43:1–2 (NIV)

• Rely on God's _____ .

> *The disciples . . . said to him, "Teacher, don't you*
> *care if we drown?"*
>
> Mark 4:38 (NIV)

> *³⁸For I am convinced that neither death nor life,*
> *neither angels nor demons, neither the present*
> *nor the future, nor any powers, ³⁹neither height*
> *nor depth, nor anything else in all creation, will*
> *be able to separate us from the love of God that is*
> *in Christ Jesus our Lord.*
>
> Romans 8:38–39 (NIV)

• Remember God is in _____ .

> *[Jesus] got up, rebuked the wind and said to the waves, "Quiet! Be still!" Then the wind died down and it was completely calm.*
>
> Mark 4:39 (NIV)

The Facts of Fear

• Fear occurs when we feel out of control.

• Most of life is out of our control, so we have a lot of things to fear.

• The secret of overcoming fear is faith in God.

> *"You of little faith, why are you so afraid?"*
>
> Matthew 8:26 (NIV)

The antidote to fear is faith. Fill your life with faith and the fear vanishes.

> *¹Whoever goes to the LORD for safety, whoever remains under the protection of the Almighty, ²can say to him, "You are my defender and protector. You are my God; in you I trust." ³He will keep you safe from all hidden dangers . . . ⁵You need not fear . . .*
>
> Psalm 91:1–3, 5 (GNT)

We fear too much because we trust God too little.

> *"In the world you will have tribulation. But be of good cheer, I have overcome the world."*
>
> John 16:33 (NKJV)

What's rocking your boat these days? If Jesus is in your boat, he will calm the storm in due time.

DISCOVERY QUESTIONS

1. Look at our key verses (Proverbs 3:25–26). Share a time when the Lord has given you confidence in the face of sudden disaster.

2. Why do you think God allows crises into our lives?

3. Saying you're confident and living confidently are two different things. What does confidence in God look like for you?

4. Have you ever seen God control an out-of-control circumstance in your life? How could true confidence that God is in control help you deal with a current crisis?

LIVING ON PURPOSE

Worship

When we are in a crisis, often the last thing we feel like doing is worshiping God. Yet it's the response he most desires. As we learned in this lesson, refocusing on God's closeness changes our perspective, and nothing draws us closer to God than worship. Take time in your group right now to praise God for his goodness and mercy. If you are experiencing a life crisis now, admit your helplessness and surrender your situation into his hands.

Look at this list of God's names.

Comforter	Counselor	Defender	Reconciler	Hiding Place
Redeemer	Healer	Rewarder	Savior	Prince of Peace
Provider	Shepherd	Father	Friend	Rebuilder
Rock	King	Restorer	Protector	_____ other

Circle the name that most fits a storm you are facing. Each day this week, tell God why that name means so much to you. Whenever you start to fear or lose confidence, remind yourself of who God is, and call on him by that name.

Fellowship

Add an extra week to this study for a potluck and to enjoy one another's company.

PRAYER DIRECTION

Take a few minutes to share with one another any storms you may currently be facing. Pray together for God to calm those storms. Thank Jesus for his presence with you now.

PUTTING IT INTO PRACTICE

Rick said, "We fear too much because we trust too little." In what area of your life are you experiencing fear right now? We all have places where fear trips us up. So what can we do to make sure Jesus is "in the boat" with us?

- What is one thing you can do this week to refocus on God's closeness? It will likely mean giving something up in order to spend time with Jesus.

- What would remind you he cares? Sometimes God's presence is found in reaching out to someone else.

- Where do you need convincing that God is in control? It might mean letting go of a situation you have been trying to manipulate.

DIVING DEEPER

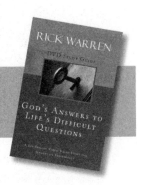

Read chapter 8 of *God's Answers to Life's Difficult Questions*.

NOTES

How Can I
Live Above Average?

CATCHING UP

- What did you do this past week that helped you focus on God's closeness?

- What new insight has God given you through this series?

KEY VERSES

If you want favor with both God and man, and a reputation for good judgment and common sense, then trust the Lord completely . . . In everything you do, put God first, and he will direct you and crown your efforts with success.

Proverbs 3:4–6 (LB)

Watch the video now and fill in the blanks in this lesson outline. Refer back to the outline during your discussion time.

SESSION FOUR

How Can I
Live Above Average?

Introduction

We all want to make a name for ourselves. We all want to be respected. We all want to live above average. So what kind of name are you making for yourself.

> *A good name is more desirable than great riches; to be esteemed is better than silver or gold.*
>
> Proverbs 22:1 (NIV)

> *A good reputation is [better] than the most expensive perfume.*
>
> Ecclesiastes 7:1 (LB)

> *Man looks at the outward appearance, but God looks at the heart.*
>
> 1 Samuel 16:7 (NIV)

How to Earn Respect

1. Respect Is Earned through _____

> *Respected people do not tell lies . . .*
>
> Proverbs 17:7 (GNT)

The man of integrity walks securely, but he who takes crooked paths will be found out.

Proverbs 10:9 (NIV)

It is a wonderful heritage to have an honest father.

Proverbs 20:7 (LB)

2. Respect Is Earned through _____

Arrogance will bring your downfall, but if you are humble, you will be respected.

Proverbs 29:23 (GNT)

Clothe yourselves with humility toward one another, because, "God opposes the proud but gives grace to the humble."

1 Peter 5:5 (NIV)

. . . before honor comes humility.

Proverbs 15:33 (NASB)

Pride goes before destruction, a haughty spirit before a fall.

Proverbs 16:18 (NIV)

Anyone who listens to correction is respected.

Proverbs 13:18 (GNT)

3. Respect Is Earned through _____

Like clouds and wind without rain is a man who boasts of gifts he does not give.

Proverbs 25:14 (NIV)

[4][He] who keeps his oath even when it hurts [5]. . . will never be shaken.

Psalm 15:4–5 (NIV)

4. Respect Is Earned through Living by _____

> *If your goals are good, you will be respected.*
>
> Proverbs 11:27 (GNT)

> *You will earn the trust and respect of others if you work for good.*
>
> Proverbs 14:22 (GNT)

5. Respect Is Earned through _____

> *He who gives generously to the needy, and [shows] kindness . . . will be powerful and respected.*
>
> Psalm 112:9 (GNT)

No one is ever respected for something they've received. They are respected and honored for what they have given.

6. Respect Is Earned through _____

> *4, 5If you want favor with both God and man, and a reputation for good judgment and common sense, then trust the Lord completely. . . . 6In everything you do, put God first, and he will direct you and crown your efforts with success.*
>
> Proverbs 3:4–6 (LB)

Spirituality not only brings favor with God, it also brings favor with man. It gives you a reputation. People are naturally drawn to those who genuinely love God and put God first in every area of their lives.

> *Good people will be remembered as a blessing, but the wicked will soon be forgotten.*
>
> Proverbs 10:7 (GNT)

DISCOVERY QUESTIONS

1. Our key verses (Proverbs 3:4–6) tell us we can find favor with both God and man when we trust the Lord completely and put him first in all we do. How have you seen God crown your efforts with success, and what have those landmark moments taught you about trusting God?

2. Look at the six qualities we reviewed. Tell the group about someone you know who demonstrates at least one of these qualities. How does that person inspire you?

3. Why do you think a good reputation is necessary for living a life above average?

4. Which of these six qualities would you like to see developed more fully in your life? Explain.

LIVING ON PURPOSE

Evangelism

Sharing Christ with others in need takes on many forms, from answering questions to meeting a physical need. How could your group become known for generous giving to others? Spend a few minutes talking about something you could all do together to begin (or continue) building a reputation for living above average. Write down the ideas you generate and commit to acting on at least one of them this coming month.

PRAYER DIRECTION

As a group, pray to become people of integrity. Ask God to help each of you be open to correction, to have a reputation for honesty and generosity, to be able to live by priority, and to live a life that counts. Pray that God will make you spiritual men and women, putting him first in every area of your lives and trusting him completely.

PUTTING IT INTO PRACTICE

Look back at Discovery Question #4. Where did you sense God tugging at your heart?

- If it's integrity, practice being more truthful this coming week.

- If you recognize a need for more humility, ask for courage to let your weaknesses show. Practice an attitude of servanthood.

- Are you generally less than dependable? Make a pledge to God to be more consistent. Show up when you are expected; be on time.

- Are priorities an issue? Ask God to help you recognize what is truly important. Plan your activities using a calendar and then surrender that calendar to God.

- If you desire a more generous heart, ask God to reveal to you this week what he would have you give to whom and where. Then be willing to give it.

- Do you consider yourself a spiritual person? How can you be sure you are putting God first in every area of your life?

DIVING DEEPER

Read chapter 4 of *God's Answers to Life's Difficult Questions*.

HOW CAN I
OVERCOME LONELINESS?

CATCHING UP

- How did you do this past week on following through with the commitments you made in our last session?

- Share an area where you currently feel or have experienced loneliness.

KEY VERSE

"I will never leave you nor forsake you."
Hebrews 13:5 (NKJV)

Watch the video now and fill in the blanks in your outline. Refer back to the outline during your discussion time.

How Can I Overcome Loneliness?

Introduction

Sociologists tell us the most common emotional pain in our society is loneliness. There are telltale signs everywhere—from call-in chat lines to blog pages to beer commercials selling false fellowship. The fact is, God made us to need each other.

> *"It is not good for the man to be alone."*
>
> Genesis 2:18 (NIV)

God's Three Remedies for the Pain of Loneliness

1. His _____ to Live For

When you're focusing on God's plan for your life, you don't have a lot of time to feel lonely.

2. His _____ to Live With

> *God sets the lonely in families . . .*
>
> Psalm 68:6 (NIV)

The church is the family of God.

3. His _____ to Live In

> *Where can I go from your Spirit? Where can I flee from your presence?*
>
> Psalm 139:7 (NIV)

> *"I will never leave you nor forsake you."*
>
> Hebrews 13:5 (NKJV)

FOUR BENEFITS OF GOD'S PRESENCE

1. He'll _____ You Out

> *"Don't worry, because I am with you. Don't be afraid, because I am your God. I will make you strong and will help you; I will support you . . ."*
>
> Isaiah 41:10 (NCV)

If God is with you and you sense his presence, you may be alone but you'll never be lonely. Remember that God says, "I will never abandon you."

> *If my father and mother leave me, the LORD will take me in.*
>
> Psalm 27:10 (NCV)

> *. . . God never abandons us.*
>
> 2 Corinthians 4:9 (LB)

2. He'll _____ You Down

> *I will lie down in peace and sleep, for though I am alone, O Lord, you will keep me safe.*
>
> Psalm 4:8 (LB)

> *You protect them by your presence . . .*
>
> Psalm 31:20 (NCV)

3. He'll _____ You Up

> *⁸I keep the Lord before me always. Because he is close by my side, I will not be hurt. ⁹So I rejoice and am glad. Even my body has hope.*
>
> Psalm 16:8–9 (NCV)

When you are alone you have two choices: you can focus on your loneliness, or you can focus on the fact that God is with you.

> *. . . your presence fills me with joy . . .*
>
> Psalm 16:11 (GNT)

When a person is walking in the presence of God they are full of joy.

4. He'll _____ You Through

> *When you go through deep waters and great trouble, I will be with you. When you go through rivers of difficulty, you will not drown!*
>
> Isaiah 43:2 (NLT)

Time spent alone is unavoidable. But loneliness is avoidable if you tap into God's plan, God's people, and God's presence, and develop a friendship with God where you have an ongoing conversation with him.

TWO WAYS TO TUNE INTO GOD

1. You Must _____ It

You must tell God, "The most important thing to me is to get to know you."

> *The one thing I want from God, the thing I seek most of all, is the privilege of . . . living in his presence every day of my life . . .*
>
> Psalm 27:4 (LB)

If you haven't already done so, invite God's Son, Jesus Christ, to put his Spirit in your life. He promises:

> *You will seek me and find me when you seek me with all your heart.*
>
> Jeremiah 29:13 (NIV)

2. You Must _____ to Get to Know God

Develop a daily time with God. Read the Bible and pray.

Develop the habit of praise. Psalm 22:3 says that God inhabits the praises of his people.

> *Enter his gates with thanksgiving, and his courts with praise.*
>
> Psalm 100:4 (NIV)

If you will take advantage of the resources God has offered you, you can reduce the pain of loneliness in your life. Commit your life to God and his plan for you. Then become a part of a church family. Build some relationships so there are people who know you closely. Get involved. Break the grip of loneliness in your life.

Stop building walls and start building bridges. Find a ministry and start doing something for somebody else.

Regardless of the source of your loneliness, God is with you. There has never been a moment in your life when he wasn't with you.

DISCOVERY QUESTIONS

1. When everyone else has deserted us, God promises in Hebrews 13:5 that he will never desert us. Why do you think God allows loneliness?

2. "I will never forsake you" also means he will never give up on you. Have you ever been tempted to give up on yourself, or felt others gave up on you? What does it mean to you to know God will never give up on you?

3. What helps you sense God's presence? What can you do to sense his presence more often?

4. Look back at all the Scriptures in the outline for this session. Tell the group which one means the most to you and then memorize it before the next session.

LIVING ON PURPOSE

Fellowship and Ministry

Getting involved in ministry automatically involves you in fellowship, because you're working together with other believers to meet the needs of Christ's body. If you're not already serving, consider plugging into a ministry that focuses on helping people, like food service ministries, greeting people as they come into the church service, or cleaning up after service is over. Church office volunteers are always needed and appreciated as well.

PRAYER DIRECTION

In addition to praying for one another's requests, let God know how much you long for his presence in your life. Express your desire to become his friend and thank him that he calls you his friend already (John 15:15). Ask for his help in building new relationships.

PUTTING IT INTO PRACTICE

You have God's promises to meet you in your loneliness—now what will you do to help yourself benefit from his presence? If you desire it, what will you give up in order to dedicate time to knowing God better? Consider making a regular monthly date to get away for a time of solitude with God and his Word—time in which you will simply be quiet and wait to hear him speak. Share your decision with your spiritual partner so that he or she can check in with you periodically to make sure you're keeping that date.

DIVING DEEPER

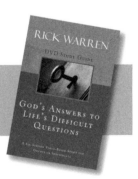

Read chapter 11 of *God's Answers to Life's Difficult Questions*.

NOTES

HOW CAN I
EVER CHANGE?

CATCHING UP

- Were you able to get involved in a ministry this week? Tell the group about it.

- Is there a situation in your life right now that has you asking, "Why me?" Share it with the group.

KEY VERSE

*As the Spirit of the Lord works within us,
we become more and more like him.*

2 Corinthians 3:18 (LB)

Watch the video now and fill in the blanks in your outline. Refer back to the outline during your discussion time.

SESSION SIX

How Can I Ever Change?

Introduction

When it comes to life transformation, what is God's part and what is your part?

> ^{12}Continue to work out your salvation with fear and trembling, ^{13}for it is God who works in you to will and to act according to his good purpose.
>
> Philippians 2:12–13 (NIV)

In a physical workout, you develop what you already have—the muscles God has given you. To "work out" means to cultivate or develop. He doesn't say you earn your salvation. He says you make the most of what you've already got. You work "out" what God is working "in."

THREE TOOLS GOD USES TO CHANGE US

1. God Uses the _____

> [16]*The whole Bible was given to us by inspiration from God and is useful to teach us what is true and to make us realize what is wrong in our lives; it straightens us out and helps us to do what is right.* [17]*It is God's way of making us well prepared at every point . . .*
>
> 2 Timothy 3:16–17 (LB)

God teaches us how to live through the Scriptures. If you are serious about changing your life, get into the Bible—you've got to study it, read it, memorize it, and meditate on it.

> *Faith comes by hearing, and hearing by the word of God.*
>
> Romans 10:17 (NKJV)

2. God Uses the _____

> *Once the Spirit . . . lives within you he will . . . bring to your whole being new strength and vitality.*
>
> Romans 8:11 (PH)

God's Holy Spirit in you gives you the desire and the power to do what is right.

> *As the Spirit of the Lord works within us, we become more and more like him.*
>
> 2 Corinthians 3:18 (LB)

God's number one purpose in your life is to make you like Jesus Christ.

3. God Uses _____

> *²⁸To those who love God and who are called according to his plan everything that happens fits into a pattern for good. ²⁹For God chose us to bear the family likeness of his Son.*
>
> Romans 8:28–29 (PH)

Nothing can come into the life of a believer without the heavenly Father's permission.

It doesn't matter the source of the circumstance, God will still use it in your life for his overarching purpose—to bear the family likeness of his Son.

> *Sometimes it takes a painful experience to make us change our ways.*
>
> Proverbs 20:30 (GNT)

THREE WAYS I CAN COOPERATE WITH GOD

1. I Can Choose What I _____

> *Be careful how you think [because] your life is shaped by your thoughts.*
>
> Proverbs 4:23 (GNT)

Your thoughts not only shape your life, your thoughts are your life.

The battle against sin always starts in the mind.

> *. . . be transformed by the renewing of your mind . . .*
>
> Romans 12:2 (NIV)

> *¹Blessed is the man who does not walk in the counsel of the wicked or stand in the way of sinners or sit in the seat of mockers. ²But his delight is in the law of the LORD and on his law he meditates day and night. ³He is like a tree planted by streams of water, which yields its fruit in season and whose leaf does not wither. Whatever he does prospers.*
>
> Psalm 1:1–3 (NIV)

The key to success is meditating on God's Word. A synonym for meditation is the word "rumination"—what a cow does when it chews its cud. That cow is straining every ounce of nourishment it can out of that grass.

- Meditation is thought _____.

> *Fix your thoughts on what is true, and honorable, and right, and pure, and lovely, and admirable. Think about things that are excellent and worthy of praise.*
>
> Philippians 4:8 (NLT)

> *Let the word of Christ dwell in you richly . . .*
>
> Colossians 3:16 (NIV)

> *⁹How can a young man cleanse his way? By taking heed according to Your word . . . ¹¹Your word have I hidden in my heart, that I might not sin against You.*
>
> Psalm 119:9, 11 (NKJV)

2. I Can Choose to Depend on _____

> *⁴"Take care to live in me, and let me live in you. For a branch can't produce fruit when severed from the vine. Nor can you be fruitful apart from me. ⁵Yes, I am the Vine; you are the branches. Whoever lives in me and I in him shall produce a large crop of fruit."*
>
> John 15:4–5 (LB)

The branch is totally dependent on the main vine. Fruit is an inside job.

> [22] *The fruit of the Spirit is love, joy, peace, patience, kindness, goodness, faithfulness,* [23] *gentleness and self-control.*
>
> Galatians 5:22–23 (NIV)

3. I Can Choose _____

You cannot control all the circumstances in your life, but you can control how you choose to respond to them. It's not what happens *to* us that matters; it's what happens *in* us that makes the difference.

> [3, 4] *. . . we can be full of joy here and now even in our trials and troubles . . . these very things will give us patient endurance; this in turn will develop a mature character . . .*
>
> Romans 5:3–4 (PH)

- Don't ask why, ask _____ .

DISCOVERY QUESTIONS

1. You may have seen the sign that reads, "Please be patient; God isn't finished with me yet." If you are worried about whether or not you can ever change, how does our key verse (2 Corinthians 3:18) reassure you?

2. Dig a little deeper—who does this verse say ultimately influences both our will and our actions? To what end?

3. The Bible says, "he who began a good work in you will carry it on to completion until the day of Christ Jesus" (Philippians 1:6 NIV). How does this truth further reassure us that change is possible?

4. Rick said, "We must work out what God is working in us" (Philippians 2:12–13). At this stage of your life, what do you think God is working in you, and what are you doing to work it out?

LIVING ON PURPOSE

Discipleship

How has God been changing you already? Briefly share the road God has taken you on to get you where you are in this moment.

Evangelism

Who do you know who doesn't know Christ and would benefit from hearing the story of your spiritual journey?

PRAYER DIRECTION

Pray that God will help you cooperate with his plan to transform you into the image of his Son. Ask him to show you opportunities to share your testimony and for the courage to obey.

PUTTING IT INTO PRACTICE

Which of the choices for change do you most identify with?

- Choosing what you think about involves a deliberate action to replace unprofitable thinking with godly thinking. Next time you find your thoughts drifting off God's course, what will you do to re-anchor them?

- Depending on the Holy Spirit requires abiding in Christ, staying connected to the vine so the fruit of the Spirit is evident in your life. What will you do to strengthen your connection to Christ so that his fruit may fully develop in you?

- Choosing your response to life requires intentionally controlling your attitude. What will help you harness your outlook on life situations and bring them in line with God's Word?

Write your responses here and share them with your spiritual partner so that he or she can help support you with this change. God does the changing, but we must cooperate with him in making the changes complete and permanent.

DIVING DEEPER

Read chapter 9 of *God's Answers to Life's Difficult Questions.*

SMALL GROUP
RESOURCES

Helps for Hosts

Top Ten Ideas for New Hosts

Congratulations! As the host of your small group, you have responded to the call to help shepherd Jesus' flock. Few other tasks in the family of God surpass the contribution you will be making. As you prepare to facilitate your group, whether it is one session or the entire series, here are a few thoughts to keep in mind.

Remember you are not alone. God knows everything about you, and he knew you would be asked to facilitate your group. Even though you may not feel ready, this is common for all good hosts. God promises, "I will never leave you; I will never abandon you" (Hebrews 13:5 GNT). Whether you are facilitating for one evening, several weeks, or a lifetime, you will be blessed as you serve.

1. **Don't try to do it alone.** Pray right now for God to help you build a healthy team. If you can enlist a cohost to help you shepherd the group, you will find your experience much richer. This is your chance to involve as many people as you can in building a healthy group. All you have to do is ask people to help. You'll be surprised at the response.

2. **Be friendly and be yourself.** God wants to use your unique gifts and temperament. Be sure to greet people at the door with a big smile. This can set the mood for the whole gathering. Remember, they are taking as big a step show up at your house as you are to host this group! Don't try to do things exactly like another host; do them in a way that fits you. Admit when you don't have an answer and apologize when you make a mistake. Your group will love you for it and you'll sleep better at night.

3. **Prepare for your meeting ahead of time.** Review the session and write down your responses to each question. Pay special attention to exercises that ask group members to do something other than engage in discussion. These exercises will help your group live what the Bible teaches, not just talk about it. Be sure you understand how an exercise works. If the exercise employs one of the items in the Group Resources section (such as the Group Guidelines), be sure to look over that item so you'll know how it works.

4. **Pray for your group members by name.** Before you begin your session, take a few moments and pray for each member by name. You may want to review the prayer list at least once a week. Ask God to use your time together to touch the heart of every person in your group. Expect God to lead you to whomever he wants you to encourage or challenge in a special way. If you listen, God will surely lead.

5. **When you ask a question, be patient.** Someone will eventually respond. Sometimes people need a moment or two of silence to think about the question. If silence doesn't bother you, it won't bother anyone else. After someone responds, affirm the response with a simple "thanks" or "great answer." Then ask, "How about somebody else?" or "Would someone who hasn't shared like to add anything?" Be sensitive to new people or reluctant members who aren't ready to say, pray, or do anything. If you give them a safe setting, they will blossom over time. If someone in your group is a "wallflower" who sits silently through every session, consider talking to them privately and encouraging them to participate. Let them know how important they are to you—that they are loved and appreciated, and that the group would value their input. Remember, still water often runs deep.

6. **Provide transitions between questions.** Ask if anyone would like to read the paragraph or Bible passage. Don't call on anyone, but ask for a volunteer, and then be patient until someone begins. Be sure to thank the person who reads aloud.

7. **Break into smaller groups occasionally.** With a greater opportunity to talk in a small circle, people will connect more with the study, apply more quickly what they're learning, and ultimately get more out of their small group experience. A small circle also encourages a quiet person to participate and tends to minimize the effects of a more vocal or dominant member.

8. **Small circles are also helpful during prayer time.** People who are unaccustomed to praying aloud will feel more comfortable

trying it with just two or three others. Also, prayer requests won't take as much time, so circles will have more time to actually pray. When you gather back with the whole group, you can have one person from each circle briefly update everyone on the prayer requests from their subgroups. The other great aspect of subgrouping is that it fosters leadership development. As you ask people in the group to facilitate discussion or lead a prayer circle, it gives them a small leadership step that can build their confidence.

9. **Rotate facilitators occasionally.** You may be perfectly capable of hosting each time, but you will help others grow in their faith and gifts if you give them opportunities to host the group.

10. **One final challenge (for new or first-time hosts).** Before your first opportunity to lead, look up each of the six passages listed below. Read each one as a devotional exercise to help prepare you with a shepherd's heart. Trust us on this one. If you do this, you will be more than ready for your first meeting.

Matthew 9:36–38 (NIV)

36When Jesus saw the crowds, he had compassion on them, because they were harassed and helpless, like sheep without a shepherd. 37Then he said to his disciples, "The harvest is plentiful but the workers are few. 38Ask the Lord of the harvest, therefore, to send out workers into his harvest field."

John 10:14–15 (NIV)

14I am the good shepherd; I know my sheep and my sheep know me—15just as the Father knows me and I know the Father—and I lay down my life for the sheep.

1 Peter 5:2–4 (NIV)

2Be shepherds of God's flock that is under your care, serving as overseers—not because you must, but because you are willing, as God wants you to be; 3not greedy for money, but eager to serve; not lording it over those entrusted to you, but being examples to the flock. 4And when the Chief Shepherd appears, you will receive the crown of glory that will never fade away.

Philippians 2:1–5 (NIV)

1If you have any encouragement from being united with Christ, if any comfort from his love, if any fellowship with the Spirit, if any tenderness and compassion, 2then make my joy complete by being like-minded, having the same love, being one in spirit and purpose. 3Do nothing out of selfish ambition or vain conceit, but in humility consider others better than yourselves. 4Each of you should look not only to your own interests, but also to the interests of others. 5Your attitude should be the same as that of Jesus Christ.

Hebrews 10:23–25 (NIV)

23Let us hold unswervingly to the hope we profess, for he who promised is faithful. 24And let us consider how we may spur one another on toward love and good deeds. 25Let us not give up meeting together, as some are in the habit of doing, but let us encourage one another—and all the more as you see the Day approaching.

1 Thessalonians 2:7–8, 11–12 (NIV)

7. . . but we were gentle among you, like a mother caring for her little children. 8We loved you so much that we were delighted to share with you not only the gospel of God but our lives as well, because you had become so dear to us. . . . 11For you know that we dealt with each of you as a father deals with his own children, 12encouraging, comforting and urging you to live lives worthy of God, who calls you into his kingdom and glory.

FREQUENTLY ASKED QUESTIONS

HOW LONG WILL THIS GROUP MEET?

God's Answers to Life's Difficult Questions is six sessions long. We encourage your group to add a seventh session for a celebration. In your final session, each group member may decide if he or she desires to continue on for another study. At that time you may also want to do some informal evaluation, discuss your group guidelines, and decide which study you want to do next. We recommend you visit our Website at www.saddlebackresources.com for more video-based small group studies.

WHO IS THE HOST?

The host is the person who coordinates and facilitates your group meetings. In addition to a host, we encourage you to select one or more group members to lead your group discussions. Several other responsibilities can be rotated, including refreshments, prayer requests, worship, or keeping up with those who miss a meeting. Shared ownership in the group helps everybody grow.

WHERE DO WE FIND NEW GROUP MEMBERS?

Recruiting new members can be a challenge for groups, especially new groups with just a few people, or existing groups that lose a few people along the way. We encourage you to use the Circles of Life diagram (see pages 74–75) of this DVD study guide to brainstorm a list of people from your workplace, church, school, neighborhood, family, and so on. Then pray for the people on each member's list. Allow each member to invite several people from their list.

Some groups fear that newcomers will interrupt the intimacy that members have built over time. However, groups that welcome newcomers generally gain strength with the infusion of new blood. Remember, the next person you add just might become a friend for eternity. Logistically, groups find different ways to add members. Some groups remain permanently open, while others choose to open periodically, such as at the beginning or end of a study. If your group becomes too large for easy, face-to-face conversations, you can subgroup, forming a second discussion group in another room.

HOW DO WE HANDLE THE CHILD CARE NEEDS IN OUR GROUP?

Child care needs must be handled very carefully. This is a sensitive issue. We suggest you seek creative solutions as a group. One common solution is to have the adults meet in the living room and share the cost of a baby sitter (or two) who can be with the kids in another part of the house. Another popular option is to have one home for the kids and a second home (close by) for the adults. If desired, the adults could rotate the responsibility of providing a lesson for the kids. This last option is great with school-age kids and can be a huge blessing to families.

What is a Spiritual Partner?

Spiritual health, like physical health, is often easier to maintain when you are working out with a partner. As you "work out" what God is working in you, sometimes you need someone to encourage you and help keep you on target. Prayerfully consider which member of your group you might ask to become your spiritual partner. We recommend that men partner with men, women with women, or spouse with spouse. Commit to pray for each other for the duration of this study. Check in throughout the week by phone, or perhaps over coffee, to see what each of you is learning and how you can pray for one another.

Group Guidelines

It's a good idea for every group to put words to their shared values, expectations, and commitments. Such guidelines will help you avoid unspoken agendas and unmet expectations. We recommend you discuss your guidelines during Session One in order to lay the foundation for a healthy group experience. Feel free to modify anything that does not work for your group.

We Agree to the Following Values:

Clear Purpose
To grow healthy spiritual lives by building a healthy small group community

Group Attendance
To give priority to the group meeting (call if I am absent or late)

Safe Environment
To create a safe place where people can be heard and feel loved (no quick answers, snap judgments, or simple fixes)

Be Confidential
To keep anything that is shared strictly confidential and within the group

Conflict Resolution
To avoid gossip and to immediately resolve any concerns by following the principles of Matthew 18:15–17

Spiritual Health
To give group members permission to speak into my life and help me live a healthy, balanced spiritual life that is pleasing to God

Limit Our Freedom   To limit our freedom by not serving or consuming alcohol during small group meetings or events so as to avoid causing a weaker brother or sister to stumble. (1 Corinthians 8:1–13; Romans 14:19–21)

Welcome Newcomers   To invite friends who might benefit from this study and warmly welcome newcomers

Building Relationships   To get to know the other members of the group and pray for them regularly

Other   _____

                             _____

We have also discussed and agree on the following items:

Child Care   _____

Starting Time   _____

Ending Time   _____

If you haven't already done so, take a few minutes to fill out the Small Group Calendar on page 80.

CIRCLES OF LIFE:
SMALL GROUP CONNECTIONS

DISCOVER WHO YOU CAN
CONNECT IN COMMUNITY

Use this chart to help carry out one of the values in the Group Guidelines, to "Welcome Newcomers."

"Follow me, and I will make you fishers of men."
(Matthew 4:19 KJV)

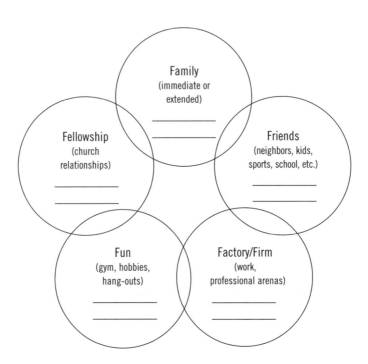

Follow this simple three-step process:

1. List one to two people in each circle.

2. Prayerfully select one person or couple from your list and tell your group about them.

3. Give them a call and invite them to your next meeting. Over 50 percent of those invited to a small group say, "Yes!"

SMALL GROUP PRAYER AND PRAISE REPORT

This is a place where you can write each other's requests for prayer. You can also make a note when God answers a prayer. Pray for each other's requests. If you're new to group prayer, it's okay to pray silently or to pray by using just one sentence:

"God, please help _____ to _____ ."

DATE	PERSON	PRAYER REQUEST	PRAISE REPORT

SMALL GROUP PRAYER AND PRAISE REPORT

DATE	PERSON	PRAYER REQUEST	PRAISE REPORT

Small Group Prayer and Praise Report

DATE	PERSON	PRAYER REQUEST	PRAISE REPORT

SMALL GROUP PRAYER AND PRAISE REPORT

DATE	PERSON	PRAYER REQUEST	PRAISE REPORT

SMALL GROUP CALENDAR

Healthy groups share responsibilities and group ownership. It might take some time for this to develop. Shared ownership ensures that responsibility for the group doesn't fall to one person. Use the calendar to keep track of social events, mission projects, birthdays, or days off. Complete this calendar at your first or second meeting. Planning ahead will increase attendance and shared ownership.

DATE	LESSON	LOCATION	FACILITATOR	SNACK OR MEAL
10/22	Session 2	Steve & Laura	Bill Jones	John & Alice

ANSWER KEY

Session One

1. <u>Come</u> to Jesus
   - This is <u>soul rest</u>.
   - The antidote for an overloaded soul is a <u>person</u>.

2. <u>Take Up</u> His Yoke
   - A yoke is a symbol of <u>partnership</u>.
   - A yoke is a symbol of <u>control</u>.
   - . . . you move together in the same <u>direction</u> and at the same <u>pace</u>.

3. <u>Learn</u> to Trust
   - Jesus' secret of peace: <u>humble obedience</u> to the Father.

Session Two

1. Remember <u>Everyone Fails</u>
2. Remember Failure Is <u>Not Final</u>
3. Recognize the <u>Benefits</u> of Failure
   - Failure <u>educates us</u>.
   - Failure develops <u>our skills</u>.
   - Failure helps us <u>discover our true talent</u>.
   - Failure makes us <u>less judgmental</u>.
4. <u>Re-Define</u> Failure
5. <u>Stop Comparing</u> Yourself to Others
6. Replace Fear with <u>Faith in Christ</u>

ANSWER KEY, continued . . .

Session Three

1. Crises Are <u>Inevitable</u>
2. Crises Are <u>Variable</u>
3. Crises Are <u>Impartial</u>
4. Crises Are <u>Unpredictable</u>
5. I Can <u>Choose My Response</u> to Crises
   - Refocus on <u>God's closeness</u>.
   - Rely on God's <u>care</u>.
   - Remember God is in <u>control</u>.

Session Four

1. Respect Is Earned through <u>Integrity</u>
2. Respect Is Earned through <u>Humility</u>
3. Respect Is Earned through <u>Dependability</u>
4. Respect Is Earned through Living by <u>Priorities</u>
5. Respect Is Earned through <u>Generosity</u>
6. Respect Is Earned through <u>Spirituality</u>

Session Five

1. His <u>Plan</u> to Live For
2. His <u>People</u> to Live With
3. His <u>Presence</u> to Live In

Four Benefits of God's Presence:

1. He'll <u>Help</u> You Out
2. He'll <u>Calm</u> You Down
3. He'll <u>Cheer</u> You Up
4. He'll <u>See</u> You Through

Two Ways to Tune into God:

1. You Must <u>Desire</u> It
2. You Must <u>Dedicate Time</u> to Get to Know God

Session Six

1. God Uses the <u>Bible</u>
2. God Uses the <u>Holy Spirit</u>
3. God Uses <u>Circumstances</u>

Three Ways I Can Cooperate with God:

1. I Can Choose What I <u>Think About</u>
   • Meditation is thought <u>digestion</u>.
2. I Can Choose to <u>Depend on the Holy Spirit</u>
3. I Can Choose <u>My Response to Life</u>

   • Don't ask why, ask <u>what</u>.

KEY VERSES

*I have hidden your word in my heart
that I might not sin against you.*
Psalm 119:11 (NIV)

One of the most effective ways to drive deeply into our lives the principles we are learning in this series is to memorize key Scriptures. For many, memorization is a new concept or one that has been difficult in the past. We encourage you to stretch yourself and try to memorize the four key verses from this study. If possible, memorize these as a group and make them part of your group time. You may cut these apart and carry them in your wallet.

Session One

Cast your cares on the LORD and he will sustain you; he will never let the righteous fall.

Psalm 55:22 (NIV)

Session Two

And we know that in all things God works for the good of those who love him . . .

Romans 8:28 (NIV)

Session Three

Have no fear of sudden disaster . . . for the LORD will be your confidence . . .

Proverbs 3:25–26 (NIV)

Session Four

If you want favor with both God and man, and a reputation for good judgment and common sense, then trust the Lord completely . . . In everything you do, put God first, and he will direct you and crown your efforts with success.

Proverbs 3:4–6 (LB)

Session Five

"I will never leave you nor forsake you."

Hebrews 13:5 (NKJV)

Session Six

As the Spirit of the Lord works within us, we become more and more like him.

2 Corinthians 3:18 (LB)

FOUNDATIONS:
11 CORE TRUTHS TO BUILD YOUR LIFE ON

Taught by Tom Holladay and Kay Warren

Foundations is a series of 11 four-week video studies covering the most important, foundational doctrines of the Christian faith. Study topics include:

The Bible—This study focuses on where the Bible came from, why it can be trusted, and how it can change your life.

DVD Study Guide: 978-0-310-27670-8
DVD: 978-0-310-27669-2

God—This study focuses not just on facts about God, but on how to know God himself in a more powerful and personal way.

DVD Study Guide: 978-0-310-27672-2
DVD: 978-0-310-27671-5

Jesus—As we look at what the Bible says about the person of Christ, we do so as people who are developing a lifelong relationship with Jesus.

DVD Study Guide: 978-0-310-27674-6
DVD: 978-0-310-27673-9

The Holy Spirit—This study focuses on the person, the presence, and the power of the Holy Spirit, and how you can be filled with the Holy Spirit on a daily basis.

DVD Study Guide: 978-0-310-27676-0
DVD: 978-0-310-27675-3

Creation—Each of us was personally created by a loving God. This study does not shy away from the great scientific and theological arguments that surround the creation/evolution debate. However, you will find the goal of this study is deepening your awareness of God as your Creator.

DVD Study Guide: 978-0-310-27678-4
DVD: 978-0-310-27677-7

Salvation—This study focuses on God's solution to man's need for salvation, what Jesus Christ did for us on the cross, and the assurance and security of God's love and provision for eternity.

DVD Study Guide: 978-0-310-27682-1
DVD: 978-0-310-27679-1

Sanctification—This study focuses on the two natures of the Christian. We'll see the difference between grace and law, and how these two things work in our lives.

DVD Study Guide: 978-0-310-27684-5
DVD: 978-0-310-27683-8

Good and Evil—Why do bad things happen to good people? Through this study we'll see how and why God continues to allow evil to exist. The ultimate goal is to build up our faith and relationship with God as we wrestle with these difficult questions.

DVD Study Guide: 978-0-310-27687-6
DVD: 978-0-310-27686-9

The Afterlife—The Bible does not answer all the questions we have about what happens to us after we die; however, this study deals with what the Bible does tell us. This important study gives us hope and helps us move from a focus on the here and now to a focus on eternity.

DVD Study Guide: 978-0-310-27689-0
DVD: 978-0-310-27688-3

The Church—This study focuses on the birth of the church, the nature of the church, and the mission of the church.

DVD Study Guide: 978-0-310-27692-0
DVD: 978-0-310-27691-3

The Second Coming—This study addresses both the hope and the uncertainties surrounding the second coming of Jesus Christ.

DVD Study Guide: 978-0-310-27695-1
DVD: 978-0-310-27693-7

THE PURPOSE DRIVEN LIFE STUDY

Taught by Rick Warren

Embark on a journey of discovery with this video-based study taught by Rick Warren. In it you will discover the answer to life's most fundamental question: "What on earth am I here for?"

And here's a clue to the answer: "It's not about you . . . You were created by God and for God, and until you understand that, life will never make sense. It is only in God that we discover our origin, our identity, our meaning, our purpose, our significance, and our destiny."

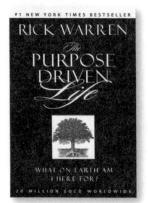

Whether you experience this adventure with a small group or on your own, this six-session, video-based study will change your life.

Be sure to combine this study with your reading of the bestselling book, *The Purpose Driven Life*, to give you and your small group the opportunity to discuss the implications and applications of living the life God created you to live.

Rick Warren

TO ORDER PRODUCT OR FOR MORE INFORMATION:
www.saddlebackresources.com or call 1•800•723•3532

Share Your Thoughts

With the Author: Your comments will be forwarded to the author when you send them to *zauthor@zondervan.com*.

With Zondervan: Submit your review of this book by writing to *zreview@zondervan.com*.

Free Online Resources at

www.zondervan.com

Zondervan AuthorTracker: Be notified whenever your favorite authors publish new books, go on tour, or post an update about what's happening in their lives.

Daily Bible Verses and Devotions: Enrich your life with daily Bible verses or devotions that help you start every morning focused on God.

Free Email Publications: Sign up for newsletters on fiction, Christian living, church ministry, parenting, and more.

Zondervan Bible Search: Find and compare Bible passages in a variety of translations at www.zondervanbiblesearch.com.

Other Benefits: Register yourself to receive online benefits like coupons and special offers, or to participate in research.

ZONDERVAN®
.com